D0854397

Smithsonian

LITTLE EXPLORER

BRILLIANT BEETLES

Melissa Higgins

raintree
a Capstone company — publishers for children

Raintree is an imprint of Capstone Global Library Limited, a company incorporated in England and Wales having its registered office at 264 Banbury Road, Oxford, OX2 7DY – Registered company number: 6695582

www.raintree.co.uk
myorders@raintree.co.uk

Edited by Abby Colich
Designed by Kyle Grenz
Original illustrations © Capstone Global Library Limited 2020
Picture research by Kelly Garvin
Production by Tori Abraham
Originated by Capstone Global Library Ltd
Printed and bound in India

ISBN 978 1 4747 7058 3 (hardback)
ISBN 978 1 4747 7064 4 (paperback)
23 22 21 20 19
10 9 8 7 6 5 4 3 2 1

British Library Cataloguing in Publication Data
A full catalogue record for this book is available from the British Library.

Acknowledgements
We would like to thank the following for permission to reproduce photographs: Alamy: Keith Douglas, 25, Nigel Cattin, 13; Nature Picture Library: Chris Mattison, 29, Jan Hamrsky, 11; Science Source/Darwin Dale, 19; Shutterstock: alexytrener, 1, Arabindu Sardar, 24, ChameleonsEye, 28, dexns, 5, Gallinago_media, 18, irin-k, 2, 20 (top), johannviloria, 9, Kazakov Maksim, 7 (top inset), Marek R. Swadzba, cover, 23, Martin Pelanek, 17, Michael Pettigrew, 20 (bottom), Michael Potter11, 15, Renat_Tugushev, 21, Ronnakron Kaewseenuan, 7, Sunsiri Meeleesawasdi, 4, TaraPatta, 27, Tomasz Klejdysz, 12

Our very special thanks to Gary Hevel, Public Information Officer (Emeritus), Entomology Department, at the Smithsonian National Museum of Natural History. Capstone would also like to thank Kealy Gordon, Product Development Manager, and the following at Smithsonian Enterprises: Ellen Nanney, Licensing Manager; Brigid Ferraro, Vice President, Education and Consumer Products; and Carol LeBlanc, Senior Vice President, Education and Consumer Products.

Contents

Amazing beetles

There are more types of beetles on Earth than any other animal. About 360,000 species of beetles live almost all over the planet. They make up 40 per cent of all insects.

Beetles crawl or swim. Some fly. Most eat other insects or animals. Some eat plants.

Beetle wings

Beetles have two pairs of wings. Their upper wings are hard like a shell. These cover and protect a second pair of softer wings. Some beetles use their wings to fly. Others don't fly at all.

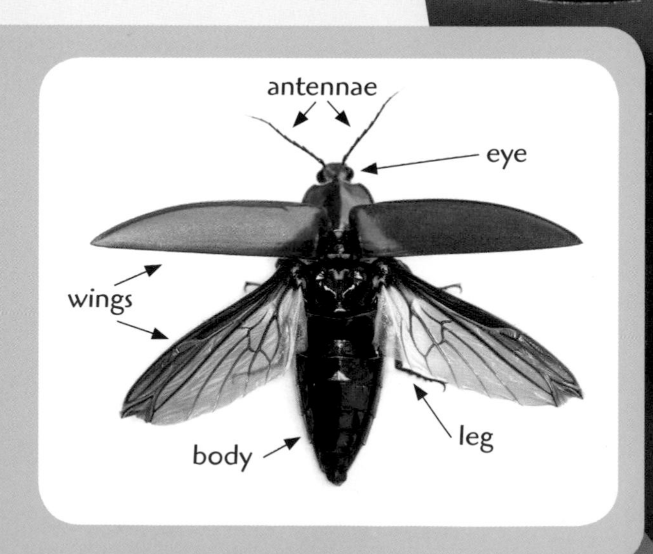

DID YOU KNOW?

The Latin name for beetle is *Coleoptera*. It means "folded wing".

Weevils

Number of species: about 40,000
Found: worldwide except Antarctica
Length: 0.6 to 7.6 centimetres (0.25 to 3 inches)

Most weevils have long snouts. The snouts have mandibles at the end. They are like teeth. Weevils use them to bite into plants. Females make holes in the ground next to plants. They lay their eggs in the holes. Larvae feed on the plant's roots when they hatch.

Weevils can be pests. They eat crops. They also get into food.

DID YOU KNOW?

Some weevils "play dead" when faced with danger. They lie on their backs and curl up their legs.

A beetle's life

A beetle begins life as an egg. A larva hatches from an egg. It moults several times as it grows. Then it becomes a pupa while it grows into an adult.

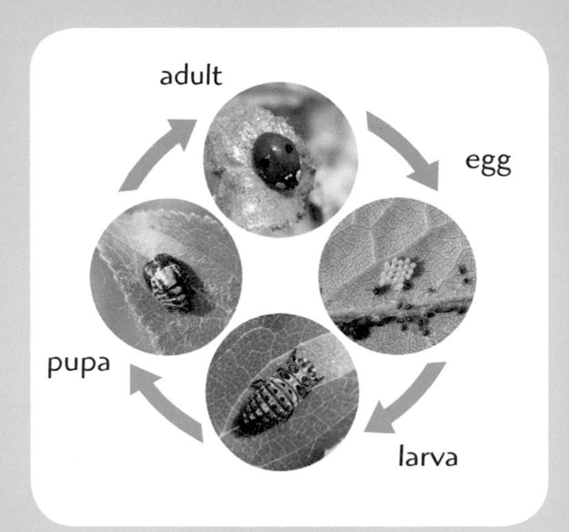

Bombardier beetles

Number of species: 649
Found: worldwide except in the coldest climates
Length: 2.5 centimetres (1 inch) or less

Like most beetles, bombardiers live on the ground. They cannot fly. Their soft wings are stuck together and do not work. These beetles have a great way to stay safe from danger. Glands in their tails shoot out a toxic spray. The spray is as hot as boiling water. The beetles make a loud popping sound too. It scares predators away.

Great escape

A toad swallows an Asian bombardier beetle. But its life may not be over. The beetle lets out its spray inside the toad. The toad coughs up the beetle. The beetle has escaped!

Crawling water beetles

Number of species: 220
Found: worldwide except Antarctica
Length: 0.2 to 0.5 centimetres (0.06 to 0.2 inches)

Crawling water beetles spend most of their lives in water. But they are clumsy swimmers. They shuffle their legs back and forth in the water. Their hind legs are long. Hairs on them act like paddles.

These beetles can stay underwater for a long time. They store air under their wings. They breathe the air while they are underwater. Most crawling water beetles live in small lakes or ponds. They eat the algae that grow there.

Skin beetles

Number of species: about 700
Found: worldwide except in the coldest climates
Length: 0.1 to 1.3 centimetres (0.05 to 0.5 inches)

Skin beetles feed on dead animals. Some are pests. The carpet beetle eats carpet, animal hides and clothes. Some skin beetles eat the stuffed animals in museums. Other skin beetles are helpful. Scientists use one called a scavenger beetle. It cleans skeletons by eating the flesh.

DID YOU KNOW?

Skin beetle larvae are the only beetle larvae covered with hair.

Tough insects

Most of the beetle species on Earth today were here 284 million years ago. That's even before the dinosaurs! Scientists think beetles adapt quickly to changes. Beetles will probably survive far into the future.

Dung beetles

Number of species: about 8,000
Found: worldwide except in the coldest climates
Length: 1.3 to 6.4 centimetres (0.5 to 2.5 inches)

What is the dung beetle's favourite food? Animal poo! Animal poo is also called dung. Inside it is a mix of plants or meat eaten by the animal. Beetles eat the dung. Females lay their eggs inside it. Some dung beetles break off pieces and roll it away. Others store it underground. Some live on top of it.

DID YOU KNOW?

Dung beetles are important. They get rid of animal waste that can harm plants and attract flies.

Diving beetles

Number of species: more than 4,000
Found: worldwide except in the coldest climates
Length: 0.2 to 3.6 centimetres (0.06 to 1.4 inches)

Diving beetles live in both streams and ponds. Their smooth, oval bodies were made to swim. They glide easily through the water. Their flat hind legs are covered with hairs. The hairs help them to float and swim.

Diving beetles store air under their wings. They breathe the air while underwater. These beetles eat large and small animals. They snack on other insects and even fish.

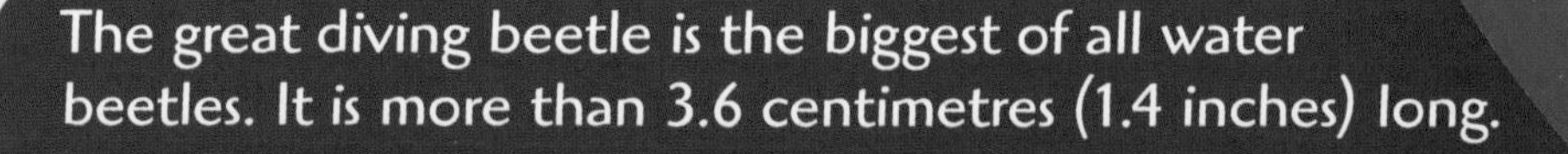
The great diving beetle is the biggest of all water beetles. It is more than 3.6 centimetres (1.4 inches) long.

DID YOU KNOW?

The larvae of some diving beetles never leave the water. They have a body part that acts like a gill.

Fireflies

Number of species: about 2,000
Found: worldwide in warm and moist climates
Length: 0.5 to 2.5 centimetres (0.2 to 1 inches)

Most beetles are active during the day. Fireflies are more active at night. Their flashing glow helps them to find mates. It may also warn predators that they have a bad taste.

Some adult fireflies feed on nectar and pollen. Others eat nothing at all. They only live for a few months. They spend most of that time looking for mates. Firefly larvae eat worms and slugs.

DID YOU KNOW?

The females of some firefly species do not have wings. They are called glowworms.

Fireflies are sometimes called lightning bugs.

How do fireflies glow?

Fireflies have a special body part that makes light. It mixes oxygen with a substance called luciferin. The mixture glows.

Ladybirds

Number of species: about 5,000
Found: worldwide except in the coldest climates
Length: 0.8 to 1 centimetre (0.3 to 0.4 inches)

Ladybirds are small and colourful. Their spots are a warning. They tell predators to stay away. Some enemies still try to attack. So ladybirds let out a bad-tasting liquid from their legs.

Invaders

Harlequin ladybirds were originally from Asia. Now they are now found all over Europe. They compete with native ladybirds for the same food. This has caused some native ladybirds to die out. One way to tell these two beetles apart is by their spots.

native ladybird

Harlequin ladybird

Farmers and gardeners like ladybirds. Ladybirds eat harmful insects such as aphids. One ladybird can eat thousands of aphids during its life. People buy ladybirds to protect their plants.

DID YOU KNOW?

Male ladybirds are a bit smaller than females. Otherwise, they look the same.

Ladybirds are also called lady beetles or ladybugs.

Longhorn beetles

Number of species: about 20,000
Found: worldwide except in the coldest climates
Length: 2.5 to 15.2 centimetres (1 to 6 inches)

Longhorns are one of the biggest families of beetles. They get their name from their very long antennae. The antennae look like horns. These plant eaters feed on flowers, leaves or bark.

The bodies of most longhorn beetles are 2.5 to 5 centimetres (1 to 2 inches) long. Some are much longer. The Titan longhorn beetle can grow to more than 15.2 centimetres (6 inches). It is the longest beetle in the world.

Antennae

Beetles don't have noses. They smell with their antennae. Antennae help beetles to find food, mates and places to lay eggs. Antennae also help beetles to know if predators are near. Beetles use their legs to keep their antennae clean.

DID YOU KNOW?

The antennae of longhorn beetles can be as long as, or longer than, their bodies!

Beetle bites and blisters

Only a few beetles bite people. Longhorn beetles are some of them. The pain from a longhorn bite can last two days. The blister beetle has another way to protect itself. It squirts out poison from its legs. This poison can make the skin blister.

DID YOU KNOW?

As many as 100,000 pines a day in the western United States have died from pine bark beetles.

Some longhorns are pests. Female Asian longhorns lay their eggs in the bark of trees. After they hatch, the larvae make holes. This damages the trees. The tree can die over time.

Hundreds of female pine bark beetles lay their eggs under the bark of one pine tree. The beetles scatter a fungus. The fungus breaks down the wood. It becomes food for the larvae. The tree can die.

Number of species: about 300
Found: worldwide except Antarctica
Length: 3.8 to 15.2 centimetres (1.5 to 6 inches)

This insect looks like the animal it is named after. A horn grows on the head of the male rhinoceros beetles. These are some of the biggest beetles in the world. They grow up to 15.2 centimetres (6 inches) long. They are also one of the strongest animals. They can lift 850 times their own weight.

Insects for dinner

People in South America and Africa eat the larvae of rhinoceros beetles. They also eat dung beetle larvae. People in Thailand snack on diving beetles. A meal of bugs may not sound tasty to you. But they can be healthy food. Bugs contain a lot of protein.

These beetles look fierce. But their horns do not hurt people. They use them for digging into soil and leaves to escape danger.

DID YOU KNOW?

Some male rhinoceros beetles use their horns to drive away other males when it is time to mate.

Namib Desert beetles

Number of species: 220
Found: Namib Desert, Africa
Length: 1.3 centimetres (0.5 inches)

This beetle lives in the Namib Desert. It is one of the hottest places on Earth. It almost never rains here. These beetles have a special way to survive. Their bumpy shells collect moisture from fog. The moisture turns into water. The water runs down the beetle's back. It flows straight into its mouth.

DID YOU KNOW?

Scientists are copying the Namib Desert beetle's bumpy shell. They're using it to make new inventions. One is a water bottle. It fills itself by collecting moisture from the air.

Glossary

adapt change in order to survive

algae plant-like organisms that usually live in water

antenna feeler on an insect's head

aphid tiny insect that sucks sap from plants

fungus living thing similar to a plant, but without flowers, leaves or green colouring

gland organ in the body that makes certain chemicals

larva insect at the stage of development between an egg and an adult

mandibles strong mouthparts used to chew

moult shed an outer layer of skin

nectar sweet liquid that some insects collect from flowers and eat as food

pollen powder that flowers make to help them create new seeds

predator animal that hunts other animals for food

protein part of food that builds strong bones and muscles

pupa insect at the stage of development between a larva and an adult

species group of living things that can reproduce with one another

toxic very harmful

Think about beetles!

1. Choose one beetle from the book. Where does it live? What makes it different from other beetles?

2. Re-read the feature box on page 20 and study the photos. In what ways are the native ladybird and Asian lady beetle alike? How are they different?

3. Use the glossary to define the word "adapt". How is the Namib Desert beetle perfectly adapted to where it lives?

Find out more

Books

Insects (Naturetrail), Rachel Firth (Usborne, 2014)

Insects and Spiders: Explore Nature with Fun Facts and Activities (Nature Explorers), DK (DK Children, 2019)

Superstar Insects (Animal Superstars), Louise Spilsbury (Raintree, 2018)

Websites

www.bbc.co.uk/programmes/articles/1pB5108szz1wyJjdpBxFS5N/9-facts-about-beetles
9 fascinating facts about beetles!

www.dkfindout.com/uk/animals-and-nature/insects/world-beetles
Find out more about the world of beetles.

Index